Hook, Line & Sinker

*How the enemy is dividing
and destroying the Christian family*

"...turn the heart of the fathers to the children,
and the heart of the children to their fathers..."
—MALACHI 4:6

Cary Schmidt

Copyright © 2006 by Striving Together Publications. All Scripture quotations are taken from the King James Version.

First published in 2006 by Striving Together Publications, a ministry of Lancaster Baptist Church, Lancaster, CA 93535. Striving Together Publications is committed to providing tried, trusted, and proven books that will further equip local churches to carry out the Great Commission. Your comments and suggestions are valued.

All rights reserved. No part of this book may be reproduced, stored in a retrieval system, or transmitted in any form or by any means—electronic, mechanical, photocopy, recording, or otherwise—without written permission of the publisher, except for brief quotations in printed reviews.

Striving Together Publications
4020 E. Lancaster Blvd.
Lancaster, CA 93535
800.201.7748

Cover design by Jeremy Lofgren and Cary Schmidt
Layout by Craig Parker
Edited by Cary Schmidt, Maggie Ruhl, and Sarah Michael
Special thanks to our proofreaders

ISBN 1-59894-021-X

Printed in the United States of America

Table of Contents

Lesson One—The Fisherman and the Fish............. 5

Lesson Two—Living Preemptively.................. 11

Lesson Three—Family Fragmentation................ 17

Lesson Four—Family Time......................... 23

Lesson Five—Putting a Fragmented
　　　　　　　Family Together Again (Part 1).......... 29

Lesson Six—Putting a Fragmented
　　　　　　　Family Together Again (Part 2).......... 35

Lesson Seven—The Wall of Protection............... 41

Lesson Eight—Responding to Biblical Authority....... 47

Lesson Nine—God's Premium on Obedience.......... 53

Lesson Ten—What Breeds Rebellion (Part 1).......... 61

Lesson Eleven—What Breeds Rebellion (Part 2)....... 67

Lesson Twelve—Internal Corruption................ 73

Lesson Thirteen—Understanding the Process
　　　　　　　of Corruption................... 79

Lesson Fourteen—Voices......................... 85

Lesson Fifteen—Submitting to the Right Spirit........ 91

Lesson Sixteen—Standing in the Gap for
　　　　　　　Young Hearts..................... 97

Lesson Seventeen—The Fear of Loneliness and the
　　　　　　　Fact of Friendship.............. 103

Lesson Eighteen—The Laws of Friendship........... 109

Lesson Nineteen—God's Plan for Right Companions.. 115

Lesson Twenty—How To Handle Wrong Influences... 121

Lesson Twenty-One—Escaping from Satan's
　　　　　　　Prison Camp................ 127

Lesson One

The Fisherman and the Fish
(The relationship between the devil and you)

Key Verse

"For we wrestle not against flesh and blood, but against principalities, against powers, against the rulers of the darkness of this world, against spiritual wickedness in high places."—EPHESIANS 6:12

Overview

Satan is your enemy and the enemy of your family. Like a fisherman, he is reeling in lost souls and even believers with his deceptive and deceitful bait. He is experienced and skilled. This lesson will introduce you to his tactics.

Introduction

_____
_____
_____

I. A __Slaughter__ from Another World *Eph 6:12*
   A. Satan is the __master fisherman__
   B. We are the __fish__.
   C. The bait is a variety of deceptive __tactics__ and __worldly__ philosophies.
   D. The bait is always __attractive__.

II. __Seeing__ the Other World *1 Cor. 4:18* / *Heb 11:3*
   A. There is a spiritual world beyond our __physical eyesight__.
   B. Our enemy depends upon our __ignorance__.
      2 Cor 4:4
   C. Pray that "the eyes of your understanding" would be __enlightened__.
   "Wherefore I also, after I heard of your faith in the Lord Jesus, and love unto all the saints, Cease not to give thanks for you, making mention of you in my prayers; That the God of our Lord Jesus Christ, the Father of glory, <u>may give unto you the spirit of wisdom and revelation in</u> the knowledge of him: The eyes of your understanding being enlightened; that ye may know what is the hope of his calling,

Lesson One—The Fisherman and the Fish

> *and what the riches of the glory of his inheritance in the saints, And what is the exceeding greatness of his power to us-ward who believe, according to the working of his mighty power."*
> —Ephesians 1:15–19

> *"For we wrestle not against flesh and blood, but against principalities, against powers, against the rulers of the darkness of this world, against spiritual wickedness in high places."*
> —Ephesians 6:12

> *"For though we walk in the flesh, we do not war after the flesh: (For the weapons of our warfare are not carnal, but mighty through God to the pulling down of strong holds;) Casting down imaginations, and every high thing that exalteth itself against the knowledge of God, and bringing into captivity every thought to the obedience of Christ."*
> —2 Corinthians 10:3–5

III. __Exposing__ the Enemy *(MIND) must be cast down 2 Cor 8:12*
   A. The battlefield is our __imagination__.
   B. We must rest in the __knowledge__ of God.

Conclusion

What does the devil want to destroy in your life? – Marriage, Family, Friends & Church

Study Questions

Teens

1. In the opening illustration, who is the fisherman, and who are the fish?

2. Why is this fisherman so good at "catching fish"?

3. What did God give us at salvation that enables us to discern the "water" around us?

4. List three ways that we are like fish. How, in those ways, are we likely to be "caught" by the devil?

5. When was the last time you sat down and thought about what your parents went through as teens? Write out five to ten questions that you will ask your parents today about how their teen life was like yours, what peer pressures are the same, and how they handled them.

Lesson One—The Fisherman and the Fish

Parents

1. Why is it so hard for your teen to resist temptation?

2. What is the devil's battleground?

3. What are some forms of "bait" that the devil might use against your teen?

4. What are some ways that you can reconnect with your teen and help refocus his heart on God?

5. List three things you can do to protect your teen from the devil's bait.

6. Pray and ask God to show you what lies you may be swallowing, and write out God's truth in each situation.

Memory Verse

"For we wrestle not against flesh and blood, but against principalities, against powers, against the rulers of the darkness of this world, against spiritual wickedness in high places."—EPHESIANS 6:12

Lesson Two
Living Preemptively

Key Verse

"A thousand shall fall at thy side, and ten thousand at thy right hand; but it shall not come nigh thee. Only with thine eyes shalt thou behold and see the reward of the wicked. Because thou hast made the LORD, which is my refuge, even the most High, thy habitation."—Psalm 91:7–9

Overview

This lesson focuses on living preemptively against Satan's tactics—anticipating his lies before he strikes. Every home needs parents and young people who will live proactively to protect themselves from the spiritual enemy of the home.

[Handwritten note:]

3 AREAS OF A CHILD'S LIFE THAT NEEDS TO BE STRONG:
1. FAMILY
2. CHURCH
3. EDUCATION

Introduction

"A thousand shall fall at thy side, and ten thousand at thy right hand; but it shall not come nigh thee. Only with thine eyes shalt thou behold and see the reward of the wicked. Because thou hast made the LORD, which is my refuge, even the most High, thy habitation."—PSALM 91:7–9

I. **Parents Are the** _Link_
   A. Teenagers need their _parents_.
   B. Teenagers need God's _truth_.

II. **The Truth** _Crisis_ **in Our Culture**
   A. It is incredibly difficult to establish _spiritual principles_ that are foreign in the home.
   B. The future of Christianity will be determined by the _foundation_ parents lay in their homes.

III. **Living** _Pre-emptively_ **in Spiritual Battle**
   A. God's Word _calls_ us to preemptive Christian living. 1 Pet 5:8
   B. Both parents and teens must live preemptively in order to _fight_ the unseen enemy.

Conclusion

_____
_____

- Teen Issues vs. Wrong Parent Responses — outcome?
- Is God a hobby at your house?
- Church can only reinforce what the family is doing.

① Research the enemy → in the bible
② Develop a defense
③ Wage a pre-emptive ~~war~~ strategy

Price to Pay
Cultural Outcast?

voice of clarity
mind of spirituality

Study Questions

Teens

1. Why do you need your parents?

2. Why do you need God's Word?

3. What does it mean to live preemptively in your spiritual life?

4. List several areas in which the devil will tempt you this week.

5. Take your list from question four and explain what you will do with God's help to preempt each temptation.

6. What are some ways that you believe God "enlightened the eyes of your understanding" last week?

Lesson Two—Living Preemptively

Parents

1. What is your role in developing your child's relationship to God's Word?

2. In what ways are you living to portray biblical truth in the eyes of your teen?

3. Why is it so important for you as parents to model obedience to God?

4. List the commands of God that you have been neglecting.

5. Describe your commitment to God in regards to the commands listed in question four.

6. Take time right now to pray and recommit to God that you will model obedience to His Word so that your child will see the importance of God's Word in your life and follow your lead. In what ways will your child see a difference in your life in the coming days?

Memory Verse

"Be sober, be vigilant; because your adversary the devil, as a roaring lion, walketh about, seeking whom he may devour."—1 Peter 5:8

Lesson Three
Family Fragmentation

Key Verses

"Remember ye the law of Moses my servant, which I commanded unto him in Horeb for all Israel, with the statutes and judgments. Behold, I will send you Elijah the prophet before the coming of the great and dreadful day of the LORD: And he shall turn the heart of the fathers to the children, and the heart of the children to their fathers, lest I come and smite the earth with a curse."—MALACHI 4:4–6

Overview

The accelerating tendency of families in the twentieth century is fragmentation. Our culture is changing and society is adding new pressures—affecting our families in a dangerous way. This lesson will encourage you to commit to your family and to stay close as you swim against the current of culture.

Introduction

_____
_____
_____

I. The __Current__ of Our Culture

   A. Life's current critically __changes__ for both the parent and the teen as the teen years approach.
   ＊ children are *still* need their affection & care
   B. The fast-paced current of life has the ability to sweep families __downstream__ to destruction.

II. The __Commitment__ To Survive Our Culture

   A. Parents must determine to hold out a firm hand of __Stability__.
   B. Young people must __determine__ to grasp their parents' hand against the pressures of mainstream society.

III. The Family __Fragmentation__ Caused by Our Culture

   A. During the last days, the __hearts__ of the family will turn away from each other.

   "Remember ye the law of Moses my servant, which I commanded unto him in Horeb for all Israel, with the statutes and judgments. Behold, I will send you Elijah the prophet before the coming of

Lesson Three—Family Fragmentation

> *the great and dreadful day of the LORD: And he shall turn the heart of the fathers to the children, and the heart of the children to their fathers, lest I come and smite the earth with a curse."*
> —MALACHI 4:4-6

B. We have **biblical** evidence of fragmented families in our culture today.

> *"This know also, that in the last days perilous times shall come. For men shall be lovers of their own selves, covetous, boasters, proud, blasphemers, disobedient to parents, unthankful...."* —2 TIMOTHY 3:1-2

C. The result of family fragmentation is **desolation**.

Conclusion

_____
_____
_____

2ND TIMOTHY 1 2

Study Questions

Teens

1. As you enter your teen years, what do you tend to do as your schedule gets busier?

2. Is your house more like a pit-stop than a home? If so, why and what can you do to change that?

3. How do you define quality time, and when was the last time you spent quality time with your parents?

4. In what specific ways can you accept your parents' helping hand of stability and learn to rely on them?

5. What activities (not necessarily bad) are you involved in that you could do less to spend more time with your parents?

6. Assignment: Sometime in the next twenty-four hours, sit down and ask your parents how their day went. Then, relay the events of your day to them as well. Make this time of reconnecting a habit!

Lesson Three—Family Fragmentation

Parents

1. What are parents tempted to do in regards to work as our kids become teenagers, and what factors influence this tendency?

2. What is family fragmentation, and what are its results?

3. What specific signs of family fragmentation is your family showing?

4. List when you will spend one-on-one time with your teenager this week and what you will plan to do together.

5. Are you spending too much time at work? What specific changes do you sense God leading you to make, and how is God leading you to get more time with your family?

6. What optional activities are you involved in that cause you to spend less time with your teen? What do you intend to do about those activities?

Memory Verse

"And he shall turn the heart of the fathers to the children, and the heart of the children to their fathers, lest I come and smite the earth with a curse."—MALACHI 4:6

Lesson Four
Family Time

Key Verses

"Children, obey your parents in the Lord: for this is right. Honour thy father and mother; (which is the first commandment with promise;) That it may be well with thee, and thou mayest live long on the earth. And, ye fathers, provoke not your children to wrath: but bring them up in the nurture and admonition of the Lord."—EPHESIANS 6:1–4

Overview

One small word sums up the countless reasons many families are falling apart—time. This lesson will compel your families to spend time together, because it is one of the most important God-given priorities in all of life.

Introduction

_____
_____
_____

I. The Family Is Designed To _____ Each Other

"And, ye fathers, provoke not your children to wrath: but bring them up in the nurture and admonition of the Lord."—EPHESIANS 6:4

A. The Bible commands families to spend _____ _____ of time together.

B. Make nurturing time a _____ and not just a _____.

C. Combine _____ time with _____ time.

II. Parents Are Encouraged To Find _____

"Hear, O Israel: The LORD our God is one LORD: And thou shalt love the LORD thy God with all thine heart, and with all thy soul, and with all thy might. And these words, which I command thee this day, shall be in thine heart: And thou shalt teach them diligently unto thy children, and shalt talk of them when thou sittest in thine house, and when thou walkest by the way, and when thou liest down, and when thou risest up. And thou shalt bind them for a sign upon thine hand, and they shall be as frontlets between thine

eyes. And thou shalt write them upon the posts of thy house, and on thy gates."—DEUTERONOMY 6:4–9

A. We are challenged to _____ God with our whole hearts.

B. We are challenged to _____ God's Word in our hearts.

C. We are challenged to _____ God's Word to our children.

III. The Family Must Make _____ a Top Priority

A. Time _____ with a godly parent becomes a _____ for every other spiritual decision in a teen's life.

B. Teens will reflect the true heart _____ a parent has for the Lord.

C. Family life is a _____.

Conclusion

_____
_____
_____

Study Questions

Teens

1. What is the critical word to remember when trying to connect with your parents?

2. With what should we combine quality time?

3. Name some ways that your parents are able to help you that you cannot help yourself.

4. List some specific areas that the devil has convinced you to close your heart toward your parents. Pray and ask God for the courage to open your heart to them in these areas.

5. How will your friends respond if you begin building a close relationship with your parents, and what will you do with their response?

6. Do you find yourself struggling every day with the same temptations? You need to reconnect with your parents and let them help you overcome them. Assignment: Ask your dad or mom when you can sit down and talk to them about your battles and let them help!

Lesson Four—Family Time

Parents

1. Does a child need you more or less during their teen years? Why?

2. What specific actions can you take to be more available to your teenager?

3. How is your child's spiritual need greater during his teen years?

4. How might your teenager respond if you try to reconnect with him and what will you do with that response?

5. Write down exactly how much quality time you spent with your teenager last week. What do you have planned for this week?

6. Spend a few moments in prayer right now and ask the Lord to help you find time to spend with your teen this week. Also pray that He will open up the heart of your teen to you.

Memory Verse

"And Jesus knew their thoughts, and said unto them, Every kingdom divided against itself is brought to desolation; and every city or house divided against itself shall not stand."—MATTHEW 12:25

Lesson Five

Putting a Fragmented Family Together Again (Part 1)

Key Verse

"Train up a child in the way he should go: and when he is old, he will not depart from it."—PROVERBS 22:6

Overview

This lesson will give your students biblical principles and practical steps that they can use to draw their fragmented family back together. These principles will combat the physical, relational, and spiritual fragmentation that exists in most families.

Introduction

_____
_____
_____

I. **Seek God's Direction through** _____

   A. Seek the Lord as you make _____ _____ in your family.

   B. Seek the Lord as you decide what stays on the _____ and what goes.

II. **Make Tough Choices about** _____

   A. Be willing to rearrange _____ in the schedule.

   B. Be willing to give _____ time a _____.

III. **Make a Week-by-Week** _____ **of Your Family Time**

   A. _____ time with each family member.

   B. Keep _____ commitments.

Lesson Five—Putting a Fragmented Family Together Again

IV. Be Willing To Schedule Extended Time with a _____ Member of Your Family

A. Get away to have _____.

B. Pray that God will _____ your teen's spirit and _____ the issues of the heart.

V. Don't Expect an _____

A. It takes time for the fragmentation to _____.

B. It takes time to _____ relationships.

VI. Look for _____ Moments

A. Nurturing is not _____.

B. _____ an atmosphere for teaching moments.

C. _____ heart to heart as parent and teen.

D. _____ biblical principles from your heart.

Conclusion

_____
_____

Study Questions

Teens

1. What specific things can you do to seek God's direction in your life?

2. How can you contribute to putting your fragmented family back together?

3. What things might you be doing that would keep your family fragmented?

4. How do you respond when your parents try to talk to you? What does this response do to your relationship and how should you change it?

5. List five ways you can show your parents that you are willing to change your family life.

6. Assignment: Write your parents a note expressing your thankfulness for them and your heart's desire to grow close to them.

Lesson Five—Putting a Fragmented Family Together Again

Parents

1. Whose responsibility is it to initiate the weekly assessment of "family time"?

2. How will reading the Bible daily help you in talking to your teens?

3. List three specific things you will do this week to draw your heart closer to your teenager's heart.

4. Write down a time when you and your spouse will sit down every week, make an assessment of the previous week, and plan out time for each child for the next week. Together commit to do this every week.

5. What are the top three things that rob consistent, quality time from your family and what will you do about them?

6. Write down at least three biblical stories of a parent/child relationship and how you could apply this to your relationship with your children. Explain how you could talk with your child about these principles.

Memory Verse

"Train up a child in the way he should go: and when he is old, he will not depart from it."—PROVERBS 22:6

Lesson Six

Putting a Fragmented Family Together Again (Part 2)

Key Verse

"Train up a child in the way he should go: and when he is old, he will not depart from it."—PROVERBS 22:6

Overview

This lesson will give your students biblical principles and practical steps that they can use to draw their fragmented family back together. These principles will combat the physical, relational, and spiritual fragmentation that exists in most families.

Introduction

_____
_____
_____

VII. _____ with the Heart

    A. Many activities do not create _____ connection.

    B. Create family settings that _____ hearts.

    C. _____ through the awkwardness of reconnecting.

VIII. _____ with Them and for Them

    A. Prayer _____ to the heart.

    B. Prayer _____ our humility.

    C. Prayer _____ the battle spiritually.

IX. Show Frequent, Appropriate _____

    A. _____ affection strengthens heart connection.

    B. Show _____ whether it comes naturally or not.

    C. Affection after _____ is vital to a _____.

X. Don't Stop _____ God

    A. _____ is not an excuse not to serve God.

Lesson Six—Putting a Fragmented Family Together Again

    B. Be willing to _____ personal pursuits first.

    C. Make _____ your first ministry.

XI. _____ God Together

    A. _____ your children to love God by serving Him together.

    B. Allow church and ministry _____ to bring you together.

XII. Recognize That Only You Hold the Power of _____ for Your Family

    A. Don't shift _____ for your bad decisions.

    B. Act upon God's _____ and make the right decision by faith.

    C. Do the _____ now—don't wait.

    D. _____ and _____ must be our first priorities, and all else is negotiable.

    E. Open your _____ to your family and embrace needed change.

    F. Be willing to give _____, as Christ did for us.

Conclusion

_____

_____

_____

Study Questions

Teens

1. What is required to create a family setting for reconnection?

2. What have you done that has hurt your connection to your parents' hearts and what will you do about it?

3. How do your parents show their love to you?

4. What time during the day do you feel the most comfortable talking to your parents?

5. Do you sometimes refuse a hug from your parents? Why? How can you change that?

6. Do you have a spirit that distances you from your parents? If so, why?

Lesson Six—Putting a Fragmented Family Together Again

Parents

1. List some activities your family might do which would not create connection.

2. Why should you pray with your teenager?

3. Why is physical affection so important and what will you do to express the right kind of affection this week?

4. Why do you need to stay in church while trying to connect with your teen?

5. What ministry can you begin serving in with your teen?

6. In what areas have you not taken personal responsibility for family struggles?

Memory Verses

"And let us consider one another to provoke unto love and to good works: Not forsaking the assembling of ourselves together, as the manner of some is; but exhorting one another: and so much the more, as ye see the day approaching."—HEBREWS 10:24–25

Lesson Seven
The Wall of Protection

Key Verses

"The LORD taketh pleasure in them that fear him, in those that hope in his mercy. Praise the LORD, O Jerusalem; praise thy God, O Zion. For he hath strengthened the bars of thy gates; he hath blessed thy children within thee."
—PSALM 147:11–13

Overview

The wall of protection refers to the God-created design of authority. Biblical authority, for both a teen and a parent, is a protective fortress—one that is meant to be accepted and exercised. This lesson will explain the purpose of biblical authority and the importance it plays in every Christian home.

Introduction

_____
_____

"The LORD taketh pleasure in them that fear him, in those that hope in his mercy. Praise the LORD, O Jerusalem; praise thy God, O Zion. For he hath strengthened the bars of thy gates; he hath blessed thy children within thee."
—PSALM 147:11–13

I. **God's _____ of Authority Is Universal**

   A. Understand that _____ lives under authority.

   B. _____ authority as a God-given part of life.

II. **Earthly Authority Will Never Be _____**

   A. _____ authority can be forfeited.

   B. God commands us to _____ earthly authority in spite of _____.

III. **Earthly Authority Is Given for Our _____, Not Our Persecution**

   "And her prophets have daubed them with untempered morter, seeing vanity, and divining lies unto them, saying, Thus saith the Lord GOD, when the LORD hath not spoken. The people of the land have used oppression, and exercised robbery, and have vexed the poor and needy: yea, they have oppressed the stranger

Lesson Seven—The Wall of Protection

wrongfully. And I sought for a man among them, that should make up the hedge, and stand in the gap before me for the land, that I should not destroy it: but I found none."—EZEKIEL 22:28–30

   A. Authority is a _____.

   B. Inside the hedge is _____.

   C. Outside the hedge is the _____.

   D. _____ are a teenager's greatest spiritual _____.

IV. Authority Is a _____ Gift from God

   A. Spiritual authority carries the _____ of spiritual battle.

   B. Engaging in spiritual battle is an act of fiery _____.

   C. Every teenager _____ that kind of love.

   D. Stop _____ spiritual authority and start _____ them.

Conclusion

_____
_____
_____

Study Questions

Teens

1. Describe in your own words God's principle of authority.

2. How is authority a source of protection?

3. Write down the names of at least five people who have authority over you.

4. Write down some rules that your parents have for you that you feel are unfair. Ask your parents and let them explain the reasons for the rules.

5. Assignment: Write your parents a thank you note for helping protect you through rules and guidelines. Tell them that you are appreciative of their sacrifice for you.

Lesson Seven—The Wall of Protection

Parents

1. In what specific areas have you failed your teenager regarding your spiritual authority?

2. For what purpose did God create parental authority over children?

3. What God-given authority in your life do you have the most difficult time submitting to and why?

4. Write out the names of at least five people who have authority over you.

5. What are some areas in which the "wall of protection" has been broken down in protecting your child?

6. Write out five rules you have for your teen. Now match a biblical principle to each rule and explain them biblically to your teen.

Memory Verse

"For this is the love of God, that we keep his commandments: and his commandments are not grievous."—1 JOHN 5:3

Lesson Eight
Responding to Biblical Authority

Key Verses
"And Samuel said, Hath the LORD as great delight in burnt offerings and sacrifices, as in obeying the voice of the LORD? Behold, to obey is better than sacrifice, and to hearken than the fat of rams. For rebellion is as the sin of witchcraft, and stubbornness is as iniquity and idolatry. Because thou hast rejected the word of the LORD, he hath also rejected thee from being king."—1 SAMUEL 15:22–23

Overview
The principle of authority requires a choice. You can choose to respond to it correctly—to experience the protection and care that God intends to provide. Or, you can rebel and suffer a life of consequences.

Introduction

_____

_____

_____

I. The _____ Response to Godly Authority

"And Samuel said, Hath the LORD as great delight in burnt offerings and sacrifices, as in obeying the voice of the LORD? Behold, to obey is better than sacrifice, and to hearken than the fat of rams. For rebellion is as the sin of witchcraft, and stubbornness is as iniquity and idolatry...." —1 SAMUEL 15:22–23

   A. _____ is one of the most dangerous positions in which we can be.

   B. God desires _____ before worship.

   C. Rebellion leads to spiritual _____ and destruction.

II. The _____ Response to Godly Authority

   A. A right response begins with _____.
   "Honour thy father and thy mother: that thy days may be long upon the land which the LORD thy God giveth thee." —EXODUS 20:12

   B. A right response involves _____ and _____ to God first and human authority second.

Lesson Eight—Responding to Biblical Authority

> *"Submitting yourselves one to another in the fear of God."*—EPHESIANS 5:21

C. A right response is _____.
> *"Children, obey your parents in the Lord: for this is right."*—EPHESIANS 6:1

Conclusion

_____
_____
_____

Study Questions

Teens

1. What is the first response we should have to godly authority?

2. Define rebellion.

3. What two things does a right response to authority involve?

4. Write down a time when you purposefully disobeyed your parents. How did you feel afterwards?

5. Write down the names of people you are rebelling against or disobeying. (Teachers, parents, youth pastor, boss, etc.)

6. Assignment: Go to the people you have deliberately disobeyed and ask them for forgiveness. Then, ask God to help you have a right attitude and to obey the authorities in your life.

Lesson Eight—Responding to Biblical Authority

Parents

1. What is God's promise to your teenager for honoring you?

2. Why is it important for your teen not only to obey you but to honor you as well?

3. What was your response to biblical authority in your own life last week?

4. How should your response to your authority differ from your teen's response to you? Should it be different at all?

5. In what ways are you striving to model godly submission to biblical authority in your own life?

6. Describe one event in your life (that you can share with your teenager) when you paid a personal price because you dishonored God-given authority.

Memory Verse

"But Jeremiah said, They shall not deliver thee. Obey, I beseech thee, the voice of the LORD, which I speak unto thee: so it shall be well unto thee, and thy soul shall live."
—JEREMIAH 38:20

Lesson Nine
God's Premium on Obedience

Key Verses

"Ye shall walk after the LORD your God, and fear him, and keep his commandments, and obey his voice, and ye shall serve him, and cleave unto him."—DEUTERONOMY 13:4

"Obey them that have the rule over you, and submit yourselves: for they watch for your souls, as they that must give account, that they may do it with joy, and not with grief: for that is unprofitable for you."—HEBREWS 13:17

"Let every soul be subject unto the higher powers. For there is no power but of God: the powers that be are ordained of God. Whosoever therefore resisteth the power, resisteth the ordinance of God: and they that resist shall receive to themselves damnation. For rulers are not a terror to good works, but to the evil. Wilt thou then not be afraid of the power? do that which is good, and thou shalt have praise of the same."—ROMANS 13:1-3

"And they answered Joshua, saying, All that thou commandest us we will do, and whithersoever thou sendest us, we will go. According as we hearkened unto Moses in all things, so will we hearken unto thee: only the LORD thy God be with thee, as he was with Moses. Whosoever he be that doth rebel against thy commandment, and will not hearken unto thy words in all that thou commandest him, he shall be put to death: only be strong and of a good courage."—JOSHUA 1:16-18

Overview

This lesson looks closely at God's command for us to obey and challenges the students to submit to God's sovereignty and to expect His blessings as a result.

Lesson Nine—God's Premium on Obedience

Introduction

_____
_____
_____

I. God's _____ on Obedience

   A. Obedience should first be _____ by parents.

   B. Obedience to parents is _____ for obeying God.

   C. When you _____ authority you are resisting God.

   D. Obedience is _____ to your walk with God.

II. God _____ Your Choices for Disobedience

   A. God created _____ to which all of humanity is subject.

   B. God determined our _____ in obedience and disobedience.

   C. God could _____ our rebellion at any time.

55

III. _____—The Place of God's Blessing

"Behold, I set before you this day a blessing and a curse; A blessing, if ye obey the commandments of the LORD your God, which I command you this day: And a curse, if ye will not obey the commandments of the LORD your God...."—DEUTERONOMY 11:26-28

A. God gives me the _____ to obey or disobey.

B. God's _____ always follow obedience.

C. Parents must _____ God's blessings upon their children by expecting obedience.

IV. The World's Greatest _____ of Obedience

A. Just as obedience is God's way of blessing, it is also a _____ way of blessing.

B. Obedience leads to a world of _____.

V. Obedience: Like _____, Like Son

"Wash you, make you clean; put away the evil of your doings from before mine eyes; cease to do evil; Learn to do well; seek judgment, relieve the oppressed, judge the fatherless, plead for the widow. Come now, and let us reason together, saith the LORD: though your sins be as scarlet, they shall be as white as snow; though they be red like crimson, they shall be as wool. If ye be willing and obedient, ye shall eat the good of the land: But if ye refuse and rebel, ye shall be devoured with

Lesson Nine—God's Premium on Obedience

the sword: for the mouth of the LORD hath spoken it."—ISAIAH 1:16-20

A. _____ should be a parent's top priority.

B. We cannot _____ what we do not know; we cannot _____ what we are not doing.

C. _____ parents have no reason to expect obedient children.

D. Parents must _____ God by being the authority He has commanded them to be.

E. Obedience to God is the purest _____ for _____ in the home.

Conclusion

_____
_____
_____

Study Questions

Teens

1. When I am in obedience to God-given authority, what can I expect God to do?

2. When I choose to rebel, what do I lose? Make a list.

3. How does earthly authority respond to obedience?

4. Describe one time that you obeyed your parents and they "blessed" you or recognized your obedience. How did you feel afterwards?

5. List some rules that you and your parents both have to obey.

6. What excuses do you use for disobeying your parents? Explain why these excuses are wrong.

Lesson Nine—God's Premium on Obedience

Parents

1. Are God's expectations for obedience more or less for you than for your teen?

2. How are you to obey God?

3. What is the result of disobeying God while trying to teach teens to obey?

4. List some specific blessings in your life that you can trace directly to God's blessing upon your life as you obeyed Him. Share these stories with your teenager.

5. In what ways have you contributed to your teenager's disobedience or rebellion?

6. What specific things can you do to help your teen grow in honoring God-given authority?

Memory Verse

"Let every soul be subject unto the higher powers. For there is no power but of God: the powers that be are ordained of God."—ROMANS 13:1

Lesson Ten
What Breeds Rebellion (Part 1)

Key Verses

"In that day I will perform against Eli all things which I have spoken concerning his house: when I begin, I will also make an end. For I have told him that I will judge his house for ever for the iniquity which he knoweth; because his sons made themselves vile, and he restrained them not."
—1 SAMUEL 3:12–13

"And I sought for a man among them, that should make up the hedge, and stand in the gap before me for the land, that I should not destroy it: but I found none."—EZEKIEL 22:30

Overview

This lesson explores some factors that contribute to and feed the fires of rebellion. Your students will be encouraged to examine their own hearts and homes to deal with rebellion at its roots.

Introduction

_____
_____
_____

I. _____ Breeds Rebellion

A. _____ is the choice to disengage from the spiritual battle for the life of your teen.

B. Nothing is more _____ than spiritual battle.
"For though we walk in the flesh, we do not war after the flesh: (For the weapons of our warfare are not carnal, but mighty through God to the pulling down of strong holds;)."—2 CORINTHIANS 10:3–4

C. _____ to God is a prerequisite for _____.
"Submit yourselves therefore to God. Resist the devil, and he will flee from you."—JAMES 4:7

D. Don't _____ in spiritual battle without the _____.

E. Eli's _____ brought God's _____ on his family.
"In that day I will perform against Eli all things which I have spoken concerning his house: when I begin, I will also make an end. For I have told him that I will judge his house for ever for the iniquity which he knoweth; because his sons made themselves vile, and he restrained them not."
—1 SAMUEL 3:12–13

Lesson Ten—What Breeds Rebellion (Part 1)

II. Rules without _____ Breed Rebellion

A. Families in modern culture are characterized by two things: no _____ and no _____.

B. Rules are an expression of _____.

C. Rules do not push teens away, _____ relationships do.

D. Teens will push rules to _____ and _____ your beliefs.

E. God's _____ and God's _____ cannot be _____—they work together.

F. Your _____ relationship with your teen will offset the pressure of your rules and guidelines.

G. We must constantly strive to _____ rules with relationships.

Conclusion

_____
_____
_____

Study Questions

Teens

1. List the first two things that breed rebellion.

2. Define spiritual passivity.

3. What are some of the lies the devil uses to get you to rebel against your parents?

4. What rules in your life do you least appreciate?

5. Ask God to enlighten your understanding about those rules and write out why your family would find it necessary to have those particular rules.

6. Assignment: Write a list of rules that your parents have for you and describe how each rule benefits you personally. Then enclose that list with a thank you note to your parents. Thank them for those rules.

Lesson Ten—What Breeds Rebellion (Part 1)

Parents

1. What does spiritual battle require?

2. What are two of the worst things you could do as a parent?

3. Describe how God's love and God's laws are the same.

4. What helps to offset the pressures of rules and guidelines in your teen's life?

5. Do you lean more towards discipline or relationship in your weekly family life? How can you balance the two better?

6. List three specific things you will do this week to strengthen your personal relationship with your teenager.

Memory Verse

"And I sought for a man among them, that should make up the hedge, and stand in the gap before me for the land, that I should not destroy it: but I found none."—Ezekiel 22:30

Lesson Eleven
What Breeds Rebellion (Part 2)

Key Verses

"And Elijah came unto all the people, and said, How long halt ye between two opinions? if the LORD be God, follow him: but if Baal, then follow him. And the people answered him not a word."—1 KINGS 18:21

"And Jesus knew their thoughts, and said unto them, Every kingdom divided against itself is brought to desolation; and every city or house divided against itself shall not stand."
—MATTHEW 12:25

Overview

This lesson focuses on two more factors that contribute to rebellion in the heart of a teenager. Parents will be challenged to consider whether they are unwittingly contributing to rebellion, while teens will be challenged to go beyond these factors and choose obedience.

Introduction

_____
_____
_____

III. _____ Breeds Rebellion

A. _____ inconsistency creates a short circuit in the spiritual development of a young person.

B. Satan will use _____ of authority to destroy the very formational years of faith in a child.

C. Until we reach Heaven, we will never have _____ consistency.
 "Till we all come in the unity of the faith, and of the knowledge of the Son of God, unto a perfect man, unto the measure of the stature of the fulness of Christ."—EPHESIANS 4:13

D. The key is having a consistently _____ heart before God.
 "Draw nigh to God, and he will draw nigh to you. Cleanse your hands, ye sinners; and purify your hearts, ye double minded."—JAMES 4:8

E. Blatant inconsistency breeds a total aversion to _____ in a teen's heart.

IV. _____ Authority Breeds Rebellion

A. Divided authority _____.

Lesson Eleven—What Breeds Rebellion (Part 2)

> "...Every kingdom divided against itself is brought to desolation; and every city or house divided against itself shall not stand."—MATTHEW 12:25

B. _____ other authorities in the eyes of your teenager.

C. Resolve misunderstandings with authority _____.

D. Be on the _____ with other authorities.

> "Two are better than one; because they have a good reward for their labour. For if they fall, the one will lift up his fellow: but woe to him that is alone when he falleth; for he hath not another to help him up. Again, if two lie together, then they have heat: but how can one be warm alone? And if one prevail against him, two shall withstand him; and a threefold cord is not quickly broken."
> —ECCLESIASTES 4:9–12

> "Now I beseech you, brethren, by the name of our Lord Jesus Christ, that ye all speak the same thing, and that there be no divisions among you; but that ye be perfectly joined together in the same mind and in the same judgment."
> —1 CORINTHIANS 1:10

> "For ye are yet carnal: for whereas there is among you envying, and strife, and divisions, are ye not carnal, and walk as men?"—1 CORINTHIANS 3:3

Conclusion

Study Questions

Teens

1. What are two more things from this week's lesson that breed rebellion?

2. Describe three areas where you have seen your parents live consistently as Christians.

3. What does Satan often use to destroy these foundational years of faith in your life?

4. What inconsistent attitudes do you have that cause your parents to intervene with discipline?

5. List two ways that you have either intentionally or unintentionally divided two God-given authorities in your life. What was the result?

6. List two times that authority stood together to help you in your life.

Lesson Eleven—What Breeds Rebellion (Part 2)

Parents

1. In what areas do you struggle the most with living consistently?

2. What is the key to consistency in the eyes of your teenager?

3. How can you reinforce the decisions of the other authorities in your teen's life?

4. List two times when your teenager, either intentionally or unintentionally, tried to divide authority and how you responded.

5. In your teenager's eyes, what ways do you support or undermine other God-given authorities?

6. Assignment: If God has revealed to you an authority figure in your child's life that you have not supported properly, go to that person and make it right, and then do the same with your teenager.

Memory Verse

"Now I beseech you, brethren, by the name of our Lord Jesus Christ, that ye all speak the same thing, and that there be no divisions among you; but that ye be perfectly joined together in the same mind and in the same judgment."—1 Corinthians 1:10

Lesson Twelve
Internal Corruption

Key Verses

"Beloved, believe not every spirit, but try the spirits whether they are of God: because many false prophets are gone out into the world. Hereby know ye the Spirit of God: Every spirit that confesseth that Jesus Christ is come in the flesh is of God: And every spirit that confesseth not that Jesus Christ is come in the flesh is not of God: and this is that spirit of antichrist, whereof ye have heard that it should come; and even now already is it in the world. Ye are of God, little children, and have overcome them: because greater is he that is in you, than he that is in the world. They are of the world: therefore speak they of the world, and the world heareth them. We are of God: he that knoweth God heareth us; he that is not of God heareth not us. Hereby know we the spirit of truth, and the spirit of error."—1 JOHN 4:1–6

"Be not deceived: evil communications corrupt good manners."—1 CORINTHIANS 15:33

Overview

Pastors and parents cannot see the heart of a teenager, and this is where Satan's most powerful corruption takes place. After Satan has sufficiently divided the home and instilled rebellion, he will always feed that rebellion with corruption. This lesson exposes Satan's tactics of corrupting and controlling the heart of a teen.

Introduction

_____
_____
_____

I. Recognizing the _____ Problem

  A. We have an _____ "sin infection."
  "Now then it is no more I that do it, but sin that dwelleth in me. For I know that in me (that is, in my flesh,) dwelleth no good thing: for to will is present with me; but how to perform that which is good I find not. For the good that I would I do not: but the evil which I would not, that I do. Now if I do that I would not, it is no more I that do it, but sin that dwelleth in me. I find then a law, that, when I would do good, evil is present with me. For I delight in the law of God after the inward man: But I see another law in my members, warring against the law of my mind, and bringing me into captivity to the law of sin which is in my members."—ROMANS 7:17–23

  B. Sin is not _____ you are, but rather _____.

  C. Satan will attempt to _____ you on the inside so he can change you on the outside.

  D. _____ corruption, in time, will completely change who you are _____.

Lesson Twelve—Internal Corruption

II. Exposing the _____ of This World

A. The _____ world is more real than the _____.

"While we look not at the things which are seen, but at the things which are not seen: for the things which are seen are temporal; but the things which are not seen are eternal."—2 CORINTHIANS 4:18

"Through faith we understand that the worlds were framed by the word of God, so that things which are seen were not made of things which do appear."—HEBREWS 11:3

B. Your spiritual enemy uses devices of the physical world to carry his _____ into your spiritual being.

"Beloved, believe not every spirit, but try the spirits whether they are of God: because many false prophets are gone out into the world. Hereby know ye the Spirit of God: Every spirit that confesseth that Jesus Christ is come in the flesh is of God: And every spirit that confesseth not that Jesus Christ is come in the flesh is not of God: and this is that spirit of antichrist, whereof ye have heard that it should come; and even now already is it in the world. Ye are of God, little children, and have overcome them: because greater is he that is in you, than he that is in the world. They are of the world: therefore speak they of the world, and the world heareth them. We are of God: he that knoweth God heareth us; he that is not of God heareth not us. Hereby know we the spirit of truth, and the spirit of error."—1 JOHN 4:1-6

C. There are two kinds of spirits that _____ in our world—the Spirit of God and the spirits not of God.

D. We are "of God" and should give our ears to a different _____.

E. God is _____ than the other spirits.

F. _____ your heart from internal corruption by giving your ears to the _____.

> "Keep thy heart with all diligence; for out of it are the issues of life."—PROVERBS 4:23

> "Hear thou, my son, and be wise, and guide thine heart in the way."—PROVERBS 23:19

G. Satan wants your heart first, because it is the _____ of your life.

H. Parents and teens are both susceptible to the voices and _____ of the world.

Conclusion

_____
_____
_____

Lesson Twelve—Internal Corruption

Study Questions

Teens

1. Define the heart.

2. Describe the ways that sin is like an infection.

3. What kind of devices does Satan use to carry his message into your spiritual being?

4. How can you recognize Satan's attacks on your heart?

5. How can you defend yourself against Satan's attacks?

6. What are some ways you can let your parents help defend you against Satan's wicked tactics?

Parents

1. What are the two types of spirits that are in this world?

2. Why is Satan's corruption often hard to see?

3. What are some influences in your family right now that may be corrupting the heart of your teenager?

4. How will you protect your teenager from the influences listed in question three?

5. How can you teach your teen discernment between the right and wrong spirits?

6. What influences are you allowing into your life that draw your heart away from God?

Memory Verses

"Now then it is no more I that do it, but sin that dwelleth in me. For I know that in me (that is, in my flesh,) dwelleth no good thing: for to will is present with me; but how to perform that which is good I find not."—ROMANS 7:17-18

Lesson Thirteen
Understanding the Process of Corruption

Key Verses

"Now the Spirit speaketh expressly, that in the latter times some shall depart from the faith, giving heed to seducing spirits, and doctrines of devils; Speaking lies in hypocrisy; having their conscience seared with a hot iron."
—1 Timothy 4:1–2

"Pure religion and undefiled before God and the Father is this, To visit the fatherless and widows in their affliction, and to keep himself unspotted from the world."
—James 1:27

Overview

This lesson exposes how Satan corrupts the heart by detailing a five-step process. Each step takes the heart further away from God and family and ensnares it in sin and corruption. As parents and teens we must guard our hearts from these influences and identify where we are in this process—if we have allowed these influences into our lives.

Introduction

_____
_____
_____

I. _____

   A. The enemy always wants to enter our spiritual heart under the cover of something _____.

   B. The attraction is always a combination of appearance and _____.

II. _____

   A. The Holy Spirit rejects, resists, and warns you about the _____ entering your heart.

   B. When the warnings are _____, you become more comfortable with this invasion of your spiritual heart.

   C. When your heart has _____ to the influence of Satan, the process is _____.
   "Now the Spirit speaketh expressly, that in the latter times some shall depart from the faith, giving heed to seducing spirits, and doctrines of devils; Speaking lies in hypocrisy; having their conscience seared with a hot iron...."—I Timothy 4:1-2

III. _____

   A. Do not interpret addiction as _____.

   B. The addiction will literally _____ your life.

Lesson Thirteen—Understanding the Process of Corruption

    C. This addiction is not _____, but a spiritual addiction of the heart.

IV. _____

    A. Satan's desire is to _____ us to the _____ of this world.

    B. The _____ is reprogrammed without our even realizing it.

    C. The influences in your heart produce a _____ and _____ countenance.
"A merry heart maketh a cheerful countenance: but by sorrow of the heart the spirit is broken."
—PROVERBS 15:13

"Iron sharpeneth iron; so a man sharpeneth the countenance of his friend."—PROVERBS 27:17

    D. We must not _____ the _____ of internal corruption.

    E. A warning sign of the inner alteration is _____.
"In thee, O LORD, do I put my trust: let me never be put to confusion."—PSALM 71:1

"We lie down in our shame, and our confusion covereth us: for we have sinned against the LORD our God, we and our fathers, from our youth even unto this day, and have not obeyed the voice of the LORD our God."—JEREMIAH 3:25

V. _____

   A. Annihilation is the total _____ of any spiritual _____ and _____ you should have in life.

   B. Annihilation happens in the heart at a _____ level.

   C. Culture has become so accustomed to heart _____ that most people consider it "normal."

   "A thousand shall fall at thy side, and ten thousand at thy right hand; but it shall not come nigh thee."—PSALM 91:7

Conclusion

_____
_____
_____

Lesson Thirteen—Understanding the Process of Corruption

Study Questions

Teens

1. Name the five steps that Satan uses to corrupt your heart.

2. What is attraction always a combination of?

3. What does the Holy Spirit do to help you see the corruption entering your heart?

4. What attractive things will the devil tempt you with this week?

5. Describe what you can do to hear and heed the Holy Spirit's warnings in your heart.

6. Describe one time in your life when a wrong influence caused you to act in a way that surprised you.

Parents

1. Describe how your teenager's behavior has changed for the worse and ask the Lord to reveal to you what is influencing that change.

2. What "voice" or influence does your teenager spend the most time hearing in a given week?

3. Where does annihilation happen and where does it show up?

4. How can you, as a parent, help control the temptations the devil is throwing at your teen?

5. Describe what warning signs you are seeing that something is negatively changing your teenager from the inside out.

6. What specific things can you do this week to actively fight the spiritual battle for your teenager?

Memory Verse

"And be not conformed to this world: but be ye transformed by the renewing of your mind, that ye may prove what is that good, and acceptable, and perfect, will of God."
—Romans 12:2

Lesson Fourteen
Voices

Key Verses

"He brought me up also out of an horrible pit, out of the miry clay, and set my feet upon a rock, and established my goings. And he hath put a new song in my mouth, even praise unto our God: many shall see it, and fear, and shall trust in the LORD."—Psalm 40:2-3

Overview

While there are many "voices" in the world today that can draw our hearts away from God, in the lives of teenagers there is one that stands out above all others—music. When a teenager or parent listens to music, they are not merely being entertained. They are being molded. The message of music goes straight to the heart, and in today's culture, music is the biggest stronghold in young lives. This lesson exposes this stronghold and explains biblical principles for choosing and listening to the right music.

Introduction

_____
_____
_____

I. _____—The World's Most
   _____

   A. All music is _____ significant in the heart.

   B. All music has _____ or immoral implications.

   C. The _____ understands the _____ of music.

   D. The spirits of the world _____ from godly music.

   E. Music in culture is _____, constantly speaking.

   F. Worldly music takes _____, heart problems and _____ them.

II. Submitting My _____ to God's Voice

   A. Our music should reflect a new song after _____.

   > "And he hath put a new song in my mouth, even praise unto our God: many shall see it, and fear, and shall trust in the LORD."—PSALM 40:3

   > "For ye are bought with a price: therefore glorify God in your body, and in your spirit, which are God's."—I CORINTHIANS 6:20

Lesson Fourteen—Voices

> *"Whether therefore ye eat, or drink, or whatsoever ye do, do all to the glory of God."*
> —1 CORINTHIANS 10:31

B. Our music should be _____ from the world's music.

> *"And be not conformed to this world: but be ye transformed by the renewing of your mind…."*
> —ROMANS 12:2

> *"There is none that understandeth, there is none that seeketh after God."* —ROMANS 3:11

C. Our music should be _____, _____, and _____ songs.

> *"Speaking to yourselves in psalms and hymns and spiritual songs, singing and making melody in your heart to the Lord."* —EPHESIANS 5:19

> *"Let the word of Christ dwell in you richly in all wisdom; teaching and admonishing one another in psalms and hymns and spiritual songs, singing with grace in your hearts to the Lord."*
> —COLOSSIANS 3:16

D. Our music should be _____.

> *"Make a joyful noise unto the LORD, all the earth: make a loud noise, and rejoice, and sing praise."* —PSALM 98:4

> *"We are of God: he that knoweth God heareth us; he that is not of God heareth not us. Hereby know we the spirit of truth, and the spirit of error."* —1 JOHN 4:6

E. We must _____ to self and submit to God in our _____.

III. What Music _____ in the Heart

A. A person's _____ will always in part be the product of their music.

B. You cannot _____ yourself into a musical style without being _____ by that style.

C. Carnal music _____ and _____ the problems of the flesh until they are _____.

D. Godly music _____ the work of the Holy Spirit.

Conclusion

_____
_____
_____

Study Questions

Teens

1. What does music do to us besides entertain us?

2. What is your favorite type of music to listen to? Honestly describe what that music creates in you.

3. Why should we choose to listen to Christ-honoring music?

4. How does music affect every part of your life?

5. List the ways that you can be exposed to ungodly music without deliberately choosing it.

6. What are the benefits of listening to the right kind of music?

Parents

1. List the primary ways the devil is communicating to your family today.

2. In what ways does ungodly music affect our lives?

3. How is your teen being influenced by the music you listen to?

4. What position have you taken on music and how have you explained it biblically to your teenager?

5. List the ways that Satan might try to gain entrance to your teenager's heart without your being aware of it.

6. What guidelines will you put in place to guard your teenager's heart and when will you explain them to your teen?

Memory Verse

"And he hath put a new song in my mouth, even praise unto our God: many shall see it , and fear, and shall trust in the LORD."—PSALM 40:3

Lesson Fifteen
Submitting to the Right Spirit

Key Verses

"Love not the world, neither the things that are in the world. If any man love the world, the love of the Father is not in him."—1 JOHN 2:15

"And because iniquity shall abound, the love of many shall wax cold."—MATTHEW 24:12

Overview

Everyone goes through life submitting either to the voices of the world or the voice of God. There is no middle ground. In this lesson, we will take a closer look at why we should allow God's Holy Spirit to control our lives moment by moment to create a right spirit in our hearts. Only by the power of God's Holy Spirit can we truly become the people that God created us to be.

Introduction

_____
_____
_____

I. **The _____ of Corruption**

"Wherefore lift up the hands which hang down, and the feeble knees; And make straight paths for your feet, lest that which is lame be turned out of the way; but let it rather be healed. Follow peace with all men, and holiness, without which no man shall see the Lord: Looking diligently lest any man fail of the grace of God; lest any root of bitterness springing up trouble you, and thereby many be defiled; Lest there be any fornicator, or profane person, as Esau, who for one morsel of meat sold his birthright."
—HEBREWS 12:12–16

A. First, there is a _____.

B. The wound _____ the heart away from God.

C. The wound gives way to a _____ of _____.

D. Bitterness leads to _____ trouble.

E. Trouble leads to _____, profanity, and fornication.

F. God desires to _____ the wound.

Lesson Fifteen—Submitting to the Right Spirit

II. Pulling Down _____ through Spiritual Battle

"For the weapons of our warfare are not carnal, but mighty through God to the pulling down of strong holds."—2 CORINTHIANS 10:4

A. Parents must _____ corruption.

B. Parents must ask what is the _____ and what is _____.

C. Pulling down spiritual _____ requires a _____.

D. The Holy Spirit _____ the stronghold and _____ pulls it down.

III. Submitting Your _____ to the Will of God

"But Daniel purposed in his heart that he would not defile himself...."—DANIEL 1:8

A. An _____ of the heart is a moldable thing in the hand of God.
   "Love not the world, neither the things that are in the world...."—1 JOHN 2:15

   "A double minded man is unstable in all his ways."—JAMES 1:8

   "No man can serve two masters...."
   —MATTHEW 6:24

B. Appetites change through _____ by faith.

C. Appetites change through _____.

D. God can create a _____ for _____ in your heart.

Conclusion

_____
_____
_____

Lesson Fifteen—Submitting to the Right Spirit

Study Questions

Teens

1. What two spirits are battling for you?

2. How often do you need to submit to the Spirit of God?

3. What can God do with your appetites if they are surrendered to Him?

4. How could your life change if you made it a habit to submit to God personally every day?

5. How did Daniel establish his priorities? How can you apply that to your life?

6. What should you do if you don't like the right kind of music?

Parents

1. How would submitting daily to the Holy Spirit change your life and family?

2. How do you develop an appetite for God and for godliness?

3. What specific things can you do to help encourage and develop your child's appetite toward the things of God?

4. How can you help your teen see the results of ungodly music?

5. How can you help your teen break free from the bondage of wrong music? How can you help them stay free from this bondage?

6. What changes will you make in your life to help your teen submit to God?

Memory Verse

"He that handleth a matter wisely shall find good: and whoso trusteth in the LORD, happy is he."
—Proverbs 16:20

Lesson Sixteen
Standing in the Gap for Young Hearts

Key Verse

"For your obedience is come abroad unto all men. I am glad therefore on your behalf: but yet I would have you wise unto that which is good, and simple concerning evil."
—Romans 16:19

Overview

Primarily to parents, this lesson focuses on helping a teenager resist the voices of the world and restore a right heart through the power of God. Every teenager needs parents who will stand in the gap and help fight this spiritual battle to protect the heart. Teens should be challenged to cleanse their hearts by God's grace and fill their hearts with good influences.

Introduction

_____
_____
_____

I. Protecting Your Teen from _____

    A. _____ your own will to God.

    B. Expect that the enemy will _____ your teenager, no matter how sheltered he has been.

    C. _____ the enemy constantly.

    D. Look for _____ signs, and don't ignore the Holy Spirit's promptings in your heart.

    E. Set up a _____ over your teenager.

    F. Fill your _____ with that which is _____.

    G. Look for _____ that the enemy might use to gain _____ into your teen's heart.

II. Restore a _____ Heart by God's Grace

    A. God's _____ is greater than Satan's _____.

> "Ye are of God, little children, and have overcome them: because greater is he that is in you, than he that is in the world."—I JOHN 4:4

Lesson Sixteen—Standing in the Gap for Young Hearts

B. _____ is a wonderful snapshot of the transforming _____ of God.

C. Claim _____ and ask Him to restore your heart.

Conclusion

_____
_____
_____

Study Questions

Teens

1. What part of your life does Satan target the most?

2. What is greater than Satan's strongholds?

3. Describe a time that your parents "stood in the gap" for you. How did that impact your life?

4. In what area of your life have you allowed Satan to have a stronghold?

5. What is the right response toward your parents when they correct you?

6. What resources has God given you to defeat Satan's strongholds in your life?

Lesson Sixteen—Standing in the Gap for Young Hearts

Parents

1. What is the first step to protecting your teen from corruption?

2. Why must you suspect the enemy constantly?

3. How can you make sure that you don't miss the Holy Spirit's promptings in your life?

4. List one time that the Holy Spirit prompted you as a parent and you listened to His prompting. What results did that bring in your home?

5. What strongholds do you believe your teenager might be struggling with? (Ask God to reveal them.)

6. What will you do to pull down those strongholds by God's power?

Memory Verse

"Create in me a clean heart, O God; and renew a right spirit within me."—PSALM 51:10

Lesson Seventeen

The Fear of Loneliness and the Fact of Friendship

Key Verses

"Let your conversation be without covetousness; and be content with such things as ye have: for he hath said, I will never leave thee, nor forsake thee."—HEBREWS 13:5

"Henceforth I call you not servants; for the servant knoweth not what his lord doeth: but I have called you friends; for all things that I have heard of my Father I have made known unto you."—JOHN 15:15

Overview

Everyone fears loneliness—acknowledging this fear is the first step to overcoming it. As we examine the heart's cry for the companionship of our Lord, may we understand that we naturally have a need for friendship and the devil wants to fulfill this need with wrong companions.

Introduction

_____
_____
_____

I. Never _____

   A. The devil's goal is to _____ you from the God who will make you whole.

   B. Having _____ and fearing _____ become a driving force in young lives.

   C. You can find _____ and _____ in Jesus Christ.

II. Why Young People _____

   A. They are _____ up.

   B. They are self-conscious of _____.

   C. We all have a deep heart-level need to be _____ and _____.

   D. We all fear rejection and _____.

III. The Devil's _____ on "_____"

   A. The devil sends "chums" in at critical times of _____ or _____.

Lesson Seventeen—The Fear of Loneliness

B. *Struggling teenagers _____ other struggling teenagers.*

C. *Wrong _____ are nothing more than mutual insecurity dependencies.*

D. *Wrong friendships _____ lives.*

Conclusion

Study Questions

Teens

1. What does everybody fear?

2. In what state is your brain, as a teen? Why is it important for you to know this?

3. How do you know that you are never truly alone?

4. What is the best resource to have in handling the rejection of the world?

5. List the reasons why you should not need the acceptance of the world.

6. Explain why you should lean on God especially during tough times.

Lesson Seventeen—The Fear of Loneliness

Parents

1. List your greatest fears as a parent.

2. List what you believe are your teen's greatest fears in their teen years.

3. What specific things can you do to fulfill your teen's deep need of being loved and accepted?

4. List one area that your teen is struggling in right now and how you will be involved in that struggle.

5. What are some of the things you did as a teen to fit in? Apply those same feelings of acceptance to your teen. How can you help them stay faithful to God during this time in their life?

6. List four ways that you can stay connected with your teen during these years when they crave acceptance so badly.

Memory Verse

"Let your conversation be without covetousness; and be content with such things as ye have: for he hath said, I will never leave thee, nor forsake thee."—HEBREWS 13:5

Lesson Eighteen
The Laws of Friendship

Key Verse

"Iron sharpeneth iron; so a man sharpeneth the countenance of his friend."—PROVERBS 27:17

Overview

There are three biblical principles of friendship that every parent and teen should understand. This lesson examines these principles and challenges the students to make wise friendship choices in light of them.

Introduction

_____
_____
_____

I. **You Will Always _____ People Like You**

   A. Your core _____ and life experiences create _____ between you and your friends.
   "Can two walk together, except they be agreed?"
   —AMOS 3:3

   "He that walketh with wise men shall be wise: but a companion of fools shall be destroyed."
   —PROVERBS 13:20

   "Then they that feared the LORD spake often one to another...."—MALACHI 3:16

   B. _____ character is drawn to friends with _____ character.

   C. _____ character finds friends with _____ character.

II. **You Will Always _____ Like Your Friends**

   A. _____ became like his friend.
   "Iron sharpeneth iron; so a man sharpeneth the countenance of his friend."—PROVERBS 27:17

> "But Amnon had a friend, whose name was Jonadab, the son of Shimeah David's brother: and Jonadab was a very subtil man."
> —2 SAMUEL 13:3

   B. We always take on the _____, _____, and _____ of those with whom we spend time.

III. People Will Always _____ You by Your Friends

   A. Having a good name is your _____.
> "A good name is rather to be chosen than great riches, and loving favour rather than silver and gold."—PROVERBS 22:1

   B. A good name takes time to _____.

   C. Man looks on the _____.
> "…for the LORD seeth not as man seeth; for man looketh on the outward appearance, but the LORD looketh on the heart."—1 SAMUEL 16:7

   D. Your friends _____ your true spiritual condition and direction.

Conclusion

_____
_____

Study Questions

Teens

1. What are the three laws of friendship?

2. Describe how your friends are helping or hurting your relationship with your family and with Christ.

3. What creates that core connection between you and your friends?

4. Who do you consider to be your best friend? In what areas, good or bad, have they influenced you?

5. List one thing that changed about you because of your friends' influences.

6. What kind of reputation do your friends have? What kind of reputation are they giving you in the eyes of others?

Lesson Eighteen—The Laws of Friendship

Parents

1. List how your close friendships are influencing you.

2. What do people judge you by?

3. List two Bible characters you can use to teach your teenager about friends.

4. What signs help you discern whether your teen's friends are godly or ungodly?

5. What specific things can you do to help your teen choose the right kinds of friends?

6. Do you have a friendship with your teen's friends? Would you want your teen to become like them? Why or why not?

Memory Verse

"A good name is rather to be chosen than great riches, and loving favour rather than silver and gold."—Proverbs 22:1

Lesson Nineteen
God's Plan for Right Companions

Key Verse

"A man that hath friends must shew himself friendly: and there is a friend that sticketh closer than a brother."
—Proverbs 18:24

Overview

God has a plan to provide you with friends. His plan is well worth the effort and faith! Discovering the best path to true friendships begins with Christ—developing a close walk with Him and then allowing Him to provide good, godly friends through authorities and strong Christians.

Introduction

_____
_____
_____

I. **Choose the Friendship of** _____

   A. Jesus calls _____ your _____ and He calls you _____.
"A man that hath friends must shew himself friendly: and there is a friend that sticketh closer than a brother."—PROVERBS 18:24

"Greater love hath no man than this, that a man lay down his life for his friends. Ye are my friends, if ye do whatsoever I command you. Henceforth I call you not servants; for the servant knoweth not what his lord doeth: but I have called you friends; for all things that I have heard of my Father I have made known unto you."—JOHN 15:13-15

   B. God _____ just as you are.

   C. Jesus Christ is the only One who can _____ for companionship.

II. **Choose the Friendship of Your** _____

   A. Adults _____ teenagers and teenagers intimidate adults.

Lesson Nineteen—God's Plan for Right Companions

   B. Break through the intimidation factor and choose to build strong _____ with authorities.

III. Choose the _____ of Christ

   A. Choose the _____ that loves Christ sincerely.

   B. Choose friends who are willing to _____ you when you are _____.
   "Faithful are the wounds of a friend, but the kisses of an enemy are deceitful."—PROVERBS 27:6

   C. Choose friends who will _____ you to do right.
   "And let us consider one another to provoke unto love and to good works."—HEBREWS 10:24

   D. Choose friends who will _____ your relationship with God.
   "And Jonathan Saul's son arose and went to David into the wood, and strengthened his hand in God."—1 SAMUEL 23:16

   "I am a companion of all them that fear thee, and of them that keep thy precepts."—PSALM 119:63

Conclusion

_____
_____
_____

Study Questions

Teens

1. How does God refer to you, in regards to friendship?

2. How does God accept you?

3. Who do you look to for acceptance?

4. How do your current friends provoke or influence you to live?

5. Are you friends with the God-given authorities in your life? Why or why not?

6. Explain the number one reason why teens do not develop close friendships with adults, and what you can do about it.

Lesson Nineteen—God's Plan for Right Companions

Parents

1. Explain in your own words the "intimidation factor" between adults and teens.

2. What specific things can you do this week to overcome that intimidation factor?

3. In the eyes of your teen, do you choose godly friendships in your own life?

4. List some ways that you can encourage your teen to become friends with authority.

5. Do you have a close friendship with your teen? What is developing or destroying that friendship?

6. Who are your teen's friends? Are they helping or hurting your teen spiritually?

Memory Verse

"A man that hath friends must shew himself friendly: and there is a friend that sticketh closer than a brother."
—Proverbs 18:24

Lesson Twenty
How To Handle Wrong Influences

Key Verses

"Now I beseech you, brethren, mark them which cause divisions and offences contrary to the doctrine which ye have learned; and avoid them. For they that are such serve not our Lord Jesus Christ, but their own belly; and by good words and fair speeches deceive the hearts of the simple. For your obedience is come abroad unto all men. I am glad therefore on your behalf: but yet I would have you wise unto that which is good, and simple concerning evil."
—Romans 16:17–19

"Blessed is the man that walketh not in the counsel of the ungodly, nor standeth in the way of sinners, nor sitteth in the seat of the scornful."—Psalm 1:1

Overview

This lesson deals with a biblical approach for both parents and teens in handling harmful friendships. It clearly presents biblical principles for relating with and reaching out to struggling friends, as well as principles for how parents should help in the struggle.

Introduction

_____
_____
_____

I. The Wrong _____

"Now I beseech you, brethren, mark them which cause divisions and offences contrary to the doctrine which ye have learned; and avoid them. For they that are such serve not our Lord Jesus Christ, but their own belly; and by good words and fair speeches deceive the hearts of the simple. For your obedience is come abroad unto all men. I am glad therefore on your behalf: but yet I would have you wise unto that which is good, and simple concerning evil."—ROMANS 16:17–19

A. _____ them and avoid them.

B. Don't _____ them.

C. _____ from the wrong crowd's influence.

D. God will meet your need for _____ as you trust Him.

II. How Can I _____ My Old Friends?

A. Recognize your _____ to obey God first.

B. Understand God's way of _____ your rebellious friend.
"Take heed unto thyself, and unto the doctrine; continue in them: for in doing this thou shalt both

Lesson Twenty—How To Handle Wrong Influences

save thyself, and them that hear thee."
—1 Timothy 4:16

C. Recognize your _____ role in your friend's life.

D. Determine to be the _____ Christian influencer.
"*Brethren, if a man be overtaken in a fault, ye which are spiritual, restore such an one in the spirit of meekness; considering thyself, lest thou also be tempted.*"—Galatians 6:1

E. Recognize that _____ is an endorsement.

F. Be willing to _____ this person in _____.

G. Trust your parents' _____ and guidance.

III. Bringing Dad and Mom in on the _____

A. Adults _____ with having the _____ too.

B. Be willing to _____ in your teenager's relationships.

C. Develop a _____ teen-parent friendship that provides a healthy emotional foundation for other friendships.

Conclusion
_____
_____

Study Questions

Teens

1. How can you get away from the wrong crowd?

2. What will happen if you take a loving but firm stand against wrong friends?

3. Who should your first two friends be?

4. List three ways you can reach out to wrong friends without being influenced by them.

5. Name five of your closest friends. Which ones aren't the best influence on your life? How can you step away from their wrong influence?

6. Assignment: Write a note personally and thank five friends who have a good influence on you.

Lesson Twenty—How To Handle Wrong Influences

Parents

1. List three things you can do to equip your teen to choose good friendships.

2. List three things you can do to reach out to the struggling crowd without allowing your teen to be close friends with them.

3. What can you do to personally show your teen how to have right friendships?

4. What is the best defense against peer pressure in the heart of your teen?

5. What are three things you will do this week to be a better friend to your teen?

6. Assignment: Write out one major lesson you learned regarding friendships when you were a teen and share that lesson this week with your teenager.

Memory Verses

"Blessed is the man that walketh not in the counsel of the ungodly, nor standeth in the way of sinners, nor sitteth in the seat of the scornful. But his delight is in the law of the LORD; and in his law doth he meditate day and night."
—PSALM 1:1–2

Lesson Twenty-One
Escaping from Satan's Prison Camp

Key Verses

"And that, knowing the time, that now it is high time to awake out of sleep: for now is our salvation nearer than when we believed."—ROMANS 13:11

"Awake to righteousness, and sin not; for some have not the knowledge of God: I speak this to your shame."
—1 CORINTHIANS 15:34

Overview

This concluding lesson sums up the purpose of this entire book. We must acknowledge that our real enemy is Satan—the one who imprisons us with his attacks. His attacks are meant to produce fragmented families, roots of rebellion, hearts of corruption, and evil companions. It is through God and His grace alone that we are able to escape from Satan's prison and establish a spiritually healthy family.

Introduction

_____
_____
_____

I. It's Time for a Prison-Camp _____

    A. Teenager, your _____ are not the _____.

    B. Parents, remember you are dealing with a subtle and _____ enemy.

II. Four Prison Camps of the _____

    A. Prison Camp _____

    B. Prison Camp _____

    C. Prison Camp _____

    D. Prison Camp Evil _____

III. Sail On—_____ No One

    A. God's command is to _____ and His promise is _____.
    "Fight the good fight of faith…."—1 TIMOTHY 6:12

    "Submit yourselves therefore to God. Resist the devil, and he will flee from you."—JAMES 4:7

    "Humble yourselves therefore under the mighty hand of God, that he may exalt you in due time: Casting all your care upon him; for he careth for

Lesson Twenty-One—Escaping from Satan's Prison Camp

you. Be sober, be vigilant; because your adversary the devil, as a roaring lion, walketh about, seeking whom he may devour: Whom resist stedfast in the faith...."—1 PETER 5:6-9

"But thanks be to God, which giveth us the victory through our Lord Jesus Christ."
—1 CORINTHIANS 15:57

"For whatsoever is born of God overcometh the world: and this is the victory that overcometh the world, even our faith."—1 JOHN 5:4

B. Your enemy cannot _____ as long as you _____ against him.

C. _____ the storm by God's grace.

Conclusion

_____
_____
_____

Study Questions

Teens

1. Who is the real enemy, and who are we tempted to think the enemy is?

2. Who do we have to rely on if we are going to escape from Satan's prison camp?

3. What are the four prison camps of the enemy?

4. Do you trust the decisions your parents make for you? Why or why not?

5. What is the only way that you obtain the victory over Satan's attacks on your life?

6. What changes do you need to make to guard yourself from Satan's hooks?

Lesson Twenty-One—Escaping from Satan's Prison Camp

Parents

1. What kind of enemy are you dealing with?

2. What is God's command for every parent regarding the spiritual battle for the home?

3. What is His promise when you choose to fight the battle?

4. What are some long-term ways that you will stay connected with your teen throughout his teen years?

5. What are some specific things you must do to fight the devil's attacks on your family?

6. What difference have you seen in your family already since you began applying the principles of this study?

   (Please consider emailing your response to question six to strive@lancasterbaptist.org—We would love to hear what God has done in your life through this study!)

Memory Verse

"For whatsoever is born of God overcometh the world: and this is the victory that overcometh the world, even our faith."—I JOHN 5:4

For additional Christian
growth resources visit
www.strivingtogether.com